MERCEDES

THE FIRST AND THE BEST

by
HOLLY HAINES

THE ROURKE CORPORATION, INC.
Vero Beach, FL 32964

ACKNOWLEDGMENTS

The author and publisher wish to thank Daimler-Benz, A.G., and Mercedes-Benz of North America for invaluable assistance in compiling the technical information for this book. Special thanks are due Robert Neary, Juergen Hoedel, and Andreas Weiland for locating the photographs and arranging a tour of the factory in Sindelfingen.

Gratitude is expressed to the following who allowed their cars to be photographed and included in this book: Elton Cox for the 1972 450 SL and Amarillo Imports for the 1990 300 SL (both photos are included in chapters 11 and 14).

Thanks to Ken Parker for the drawing of Germany on page 5.

PHOTO CREDITS:

All of the photographs in this book are from Daimler-Benz, A.G., except the following taken by Harry Haines: 500 K in chapter 5; 1952 300 SL racing car, 1954 300 SL coupé, and 1960 300 SL convertible in chapter 10; 1972 450 SL and 1990 300 SL in chapters 11 and 14.

Library of Congress Cataloging-in-Publication Data

Haines, Holly, 1960-
    Mercedes: the first and the best/ by Holly Haines.
       p. cm. – (Car classics)
    Includes index.
    Summary: Profiles the history of a pioneer company whose many designs, inventions, and innovations became milestones in the history of the car and automotive engineering.
    ISBN 0-86593-142-9
    1. Mercedes automobile – History – Juvenile literature.
[1. Mercedes automobile – History.] I. Title. II. Series: Car Classics (Vero Beach, Fla.)
TL215.M4H35 1991
338.7'629222 – dc20   91-9658
                                       CIP
                                       AC

TABLE OF CONTENTS

CHAPTER 1

INTRODUCING MERCEDES-BENZ

The history of Mercedes-Benz parallels the history of the automobile. The *Guinness Book of World Records* and most encyclopedias cite Karl Benz as the inventor of the car and Gottlieb Daimler as the developer of the first gasoline engines suitable for automotive use. Benz, Daimler, and the companies they founded also designed the first motorcycle, first gasoline-powered motorboat, first airship and airplane engines, the first diesel automobiles, and a variety of other important milestones in the history of the car.

A coupé 230 CE. The familiar grill identifies the car as one of the most famous in the world, Mercedes-Benz.

Daimler-Benz manufacturing plants are located all over Germany; the headquarters is located in Stuttgart.

HAMBURG
BREMEN
BERLIN

GERMANY

DÜSSELDORF
FRANKFURT
MANNHEIM
UNTERTURKHEIM
STUTTGART
SINDELFINGEN
MUNICH

When people think of Mercedes-Benz today, they think of a finely crafted luxury car. Throughout their history, Daimler and Benz have been known for the quality and innovativeness of their cars. The company has become one of the largest automotive manufacturers in the world and now employs over 450,000 people worldwide. Mercedes-Benz factories are located all over Germany with headquarters in Stuttgart. The company is an important part of the German economy and a symbol of the country's engineering excellence.

The main plant in Sindelfingen is a large ultramodern facility that employs 45,000 people and produces 1,700 cars a day. (An additional 300 cars are produced in Bremen.)

CHAPTER 2

FOUNDERS

Two men, Karl Benz and Gottlieb Daimler, are generally acknowledged to have created the first automobiles. Their work began separately in the south of Germany over a century ago.

Gottlieb Daimler was born in 1834 in the village of Schorndorf, just east of what later became Stuttgart, Germany. He trained as an engineer. After jobs in several factories and travel abroad, Daimler retired to the Stuttgart suburb of Cannstatt in December of 1881. Daimler soon turned his new greenhouse into a workshop. In 1885 Daimler patented his water-cooled engine.

Gottlieb Daimler,
1834-1900

Karl Benz was born in the village of Pfaffenrot in 1844. His father died two years later in a locomotive accident, and Karl's mother struggled to finance his education. Upon graduation, Benz went to work in the town locomotive works and rose to the position of draftsman. He went on to build bridges in Pforzheim and then opened his own machinist shop in Mannheim. After a struggling start, Benz took on partners in 1882 to form a

1886 Daimler
Motor Carriage
1-cylinder
462-cc engine
1.1 hp at 700 rpm
Top speed: 10 mph

Daimler's first automobile, a four-wheel carriage adapted for use with the new Daimler engine.

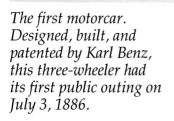

1886 Benz Patent Motor Car
1-cylinder
984-cc engine
0.9 hp at 400 rpm
Top speed: 10 mph

The first motorcar. Designed, built, and patented by Karl Benz, this three-wheeler had its first public outing on July 3, 1886.

Karl Benz, 1844-1929

company to manufacture his new engine design. Problems arose between the partners, and Benz founded another new company in October of 1883, the famous Benz & Co. (later called Benz & Cie.)

Independently, Daimler and Benz decided to build engines based on the new gasoline fuel. Once Benz's engine was developed and selling well, Benz installed it on a carriage. In the fall of 1885, Benz tested his motorcar for the first time.

Daimler's first vehicle was a motorcycle, designed and built in 1885. In early 1886 he ordered a new carriage from a local coach builder for his wife's birthday. It was to be used with the new engine as his first motorized, four-wheel vehicle, but the carriage was late in arriving. Impatient to begin, he placed his engine in a motorboat and tested it on the Neckar River. The carriage Daimler had ordered finally arrived from the coach builder, and its conversion to motor carriage was completed that fall.

Although Karl Benz and Gottlieb Daimler lived and worked only 60 miles apart and their companies later merged, they never met one another.

CHAPTER 3

EARLY YEARS

The Benz Victoria built in 1893 was the first four-wheel Benz car.

Building a motorcar and building a company are two different things. A person who is successful at one may not be good at the other.

Gottlieb Daimler, an experienced businessman, was good at both. He expanded his company into New York, Paris, and England. He enlarged his product line to include trucks, fire engines, trolley cars, omnibuses, and taxis, as well as boats and cars.

Karl Benz, on the other hand, was constantly struggling with money and technical problems. In August of 1888, when he despaired that the car could ever become useful and profitable, his wife Berta took matters into her own hands. Berta and their two oldest sons stole out of the house before dawn and took the car on its first "long-distance" trip. The 50 miles from Mannheim to Pforzheim were an adventure for the family. The car had to be

The 1893 Benz Victoria
1-cylinder
2.9-liter engine
5 hp at 700 rpm
Top speed: 21 mph

pushed up every hill, fuel was bought at a pharmacy, and problems had to be solved with items at hand. But they arrived in Pforzheim in triumph just after dark. This trip established the motorcar as viable means of transportation and changed the status of the automobile from toy to vehicle.

Benz continued to develop his automobile, and in 1893 he built his first four-wheel model, the Victoria. In July, 1894, an Austrian industrialist drove a Benz Victoria from Reichenbert in Bohemia by way of Mannheim and Gondorf on the Mosel River all the way to Rheim, France and back. This three-country motor tour totaled over 1,000 miles and proved that the Benz car was both sturdy and reliable.

By 1899, Benz & Cie. was the largest manufacturer of automobiles in the world.

Berta Benz around 1888. To publicize her husband Karl's work, she made the first long-distance auto trip with her two oldest sons.

CHAPTER 4

THE ERA OF MERCEDES

In the late 1800s, the social elite of Europe spent much of their time in Nice on the French Riviera. During the "Week of Nice" in 1899, automobiles raced to Salon and back, over 240 miles. The hazardous hill climb, La Turbie, became an especially popular spot to challenge motorists. Emil Jellinek, an Austrian businessman and diplomat, was one of the many sportsmen impressed by the Daimler cars. He purchased four of the 1899 Daimler Phoenix models and sold them to friends and colleagues after he raced past them on La Turbie. Jellinek was convinced that Daimler could provide even more in the way of power, speed, and cars. He ordered 36 cars worth 550,000 gold marks with the suggestion that the car be named for his daughter, Mercédès. The car and its name were so popular that DMG used the name for all its new models and made it the trademark in 1902.

Emil Jellinek, an Austrian businessman. He became a leading promoter of the new Daimler motor cars.

Emil Jellinek's daughter Mercédès at age 11. She became famous when, at her father's request, the new line of Daimler automobiles was named for her.

*The first Mercedes.
Radically different from the
horseless carriages it
replaced, it dominated the
automotive scene in the
new century.*

With a lower center of gravity, longer wheelbase and low-pressure tires, the Mercedes was a marvel of engineering innovation. It had four speeds plus reverse, all connected by a coil spring clutch. The gearbox was fitted with a differential, and power was transmitted to the rear wheels via a sprocket wheel shaft. The first Mercedes was a sturdy, dependable, speedy automobile. This car was not just a horseless carriage; it began a new era of automotive history.

**The 1902
Mercedes
Simplex**
4-cylinder
5.3-liter engine
40 hp at 1050 rpm
Top speed: 47 mph

CHAPTER 5

THE COMPANIES MERGE

Germany was in financial ruin at the end of World War I. The wildest period of inflation and devaluation the world had ever seen ended in the collapse of the German currency. Both Daimler and Benz had established their reputations on engineering quality of the highest standards. From humble beginnings, Daimler had moved to Untertürkheim in 1904 and established an aircraft engine plant in Sindelfingen during the war. Benz kept his works near Mannheim. In 1910, the Benz company acquired the Gaggenau bus and truck works at Baden-Baden. This expansive growth was no protection for either company in postwar Germany. In 1926, Daimler Motoren-Gesellschaft (DMG) and Benz & Cie., became Daimler-Benz, A.G. Their cars would be called Mercedes-Benz.

The famous three-pointed star symbol had been registered in 1909 by the Daimler Company to symbolize the threefold nature of transportation on land, sea, and in the air. The Benz company used a laurel wreath encircling the name "Benz" to symbolize high achievement. When the companies merged, the new company symbol became the three-pointed star encircled by a laurel with the word Mercedes on top and Benz on the bottom. This symbol is still used today.

A 1931 Mercedes-Benz 370S, Mannheim Cabriolet A. This 6-cylinder, 3.7-liter engine produced 78 hp at 3200 rpm. Its top speed was 75 mph. The Mannheim was an upper mid-range model named for the home city of Benz & Cie.

A 1928 Mercedes-Benz 260 Stuttgart convertible. Its 6-cylinder, 2.5-liter engine produced 50 hp at 3200 rpm. Top speed is 56 mph. The Stuttgart was named for the home city of DMG. It became the mainstay of car sales in the late 1920s.

Production in the new company concentrated on a pair of new cars: a 2-liter known as the "Stuttgart," and a 3.1-liter named the "Mannheim." These names celebrated the cities where each company originated. Both cars sold well and assured the success of Mercedes-Benz.

In the 1930s, Daimler-Benz began "supercharging" engines with designs by Ferdinand Porsche. These "SS" and "SSK" models helped move the company back to the top in performance and styling.

The 1936 Mercedes-Benz 500 K

8-cylinder
5-liter engine
100 hp at 3400 rpm; 160 hp with supercharger
Top speed: 100 mph

The 1936 Mercedes-Benz 500 K luxury convertible. Only 25 of these luxury convertibles were built between 1935 and 1936.

CHAPTER 6

RACING

Racing proved an excellent way of displaying the speed and reliability of the new motorcar. The first sponsored automobile race was an exhibition held in France in July, 1894; the 78-mile course began in Paris and ended in Rouen. The only qualification for entry was a "carriage without horse" – anything that could cover the distance under its own power. The winning vehicles were powered by Daimler engines. Karl Benz disapproved of racing as dangerous, but his French distributor entered the race anyway. He proved the Benz's reliability, but not its speed. The Benz came in behind all of the other gasoline-powered cars. Another race was held in 1895 from Paris to Bordeaux and back, 732 miles. Only 9 of the 22 cars completed the race – the fastest in 90 hours. Auto racing was born.

Over the next few years, Daimler's Mercedes held the attention of auto enthusiasts. Benz & Cie. was establishing its reputation as a maker of reliable cars bought by the elite of Europe. By 1908,

The Benz Phaeton, driven in the Paris-Bordeaux-Paris race of 1895 by Emile Roger, the French distributor for Karl Benz. It finished seventh – one of only nine to complete the course.

The 1909 Blitzen Benz. This 200 hp car set world records from 1909 to 1924. The "Blitzen Benz" (Lightning Benz) had an enormous 21.5-liter engine geared for 140 mph at 1400 rpm. Driven by Barney Oldfield, this car dominated the racing scene for a decade and a half.

The 1937 model W125. Designed to the 750-kg weight restriction with an 8-cylinder, 5.6-liter engine producing 646 hp at 5800 rpm. Its top speed was 330 mph.

The W196 came in two models: an open-wheeled (right) and a new streamliner. A big winner on the Grand Prix circuits in 1954-55, the W196 produced 290 hp at 8700 rpm.

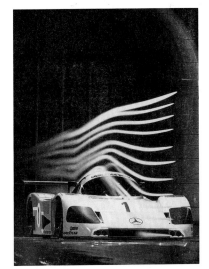

The 1990 Mercedes-Benz Formula I racing car shown in the wind tunnel.

the company had overcome Karl Benz's objections to racing cars. In 1909 the famous Blitzen Benz with its enormous 21.5-liter engine began setting records that held for the next fifteen years.

Soon after the 1926 merger of the two companies, the Great Depression limited German racing. By 1934, though, the German government was ready to sponsor racing. In response, Mercedes-Benz developed the W25. This car and the models that followed it led Mercedes-Benz to dominate racing during the 1930s.

Car production came to a standstill during World War II. It was 1952 before Mercedes-Benz returned to the track. The W196 was designed from the bottom up for the new Formula I racing. It had a straight 8-cylinder, 2.5-liter engine and top speeds of 172 mph (open wheels) and 187 mph (streamlined version). This car re-established Mercedes-Benz as an international racing powerhouse by winning 10 Grand Prix races in 1954 and 1955. In 1955, having proven their reputation, and following a terrible crash at Le Mans, Mercedes-Benz retired from racing automobiles.

In 1987 Mercedes-Benz resumed racing, once again putting the three-pointed star on the Formula I circuit.

CHAPTER 7

WORLD RECORD CARS

In the 100-year history of the automobile, Daimler-Benz has probably won more races and set more records than any other auto maker. Two of their most spectacular record-breaking cars are pictured here.

In 1938, the W125 was raced on the Frankfurt to Heidelberg *autobahn* (highway) and reached a top speed of 432.7 km/h (271 mph). This record still stands for the fastest kilometer on a public road.

About this same time the company set as a goal "the building of the world's fastest automobile." The project was named the T80. Ferdinand Porsche was chosen to lead the design team, and a super car was planned. Of the several engines tried, the one

One of the most famous cars ever built is the W125. Powered by a 12-cylinder engine of 5577 cc, it was rated at 736 hp.

The T80, the most powerful car ever built by Mercedes-Benz, was never raced. Its engine was a 44.5-liter monster rated at 2800 hp. Estimated top speed was 650 km/h (406 mph).

chosen was a monster 12-cylinder, 44,522-cc (44.5-liter) airplane engine. Rated at 2800 hp, it had four driven rear wheels to transfer maximum power to the road. The coefficient of drag was an incredible 0.18, the lightest ever seen at that time. Some early tests were run in October, 1939.

But World War II started and, one month before completion, the T80 project was canceled.

CHAPTER 8

TRUCKS AND BUSES

Although Mercedes-Benz is well known for its high-quality luxury cars, very few Americans also recognize the company as the world's largest manufacturer of heavy trucks.

Daimler and Benz realized very early the benefits of producing commercial trucks. Daimler put the world's first motor truck into production in 1896. It had a 4 hp engine. By 1898, a twin-cylinder engine, 5-ton model was unveiled at a Paris show. Daimler omnibuses became an important item in the Daimler products when the first motor-bus line opened on July 15, 1899 from Künzelsau to Mergentheim.

Aero engines, first built for the Zeppelin in 1900, later became the basis for a large business that provided engines for airplanes and racing cars. From the advent of the Mercedes in 1901, the Daimler company focused on motor vehicles – cars, trucks, buses, and engines for various purposes.

A Daimler engine powered this 1899 Zeppelin airship.

The 2-cylinder, 1.5-liter engine of this 1898 Daimler Lastwagen produced a top speed of 6 mph. One of the first trucks ever made, it is on display in the Daimler-Benz museum in Stuttgart.

The 1990 Mercedes-Benz 1748 Model heavy truck

Benz produced his first truck and motor omnibus in the late 1880s. This bus was the first used on the Siegen-Netphen-Deutz run in 1896. The Benz Mannheim works received a patent for an efficient diesel engine, named after its inventor, Rudolf Diesel, in 1909. The diesel engine was first used in a truck in 1924 and in passenger cars in 1936. Many Mercedes-Benz trucks were adapted for military use during World War II. Engines for the Panther and Tiger tanks as well as the famous Messerschmitt fighter planes and bombers were built by Daimler-Benz, A.G.

After the war, the Mannheim factory was the least damaged of the Mercedes plants during Allied bombing raids. It was the first to be restored for production of heavy trucks and buses, which were badly needed in the late 1940s.

In 1948 the Unimog was introduced. Combining the abilities of farm tractor, power plant, and transporter, the Unimog could negotiate difficult terrain and be driven at speeds from 1.8 to 43 mph. In 1990 the new SK heavy truck was voted "Truck of the Year" by an international jury of journalists, demonstrating that quality and innovation live on today in Mercedes-Benz commercial truck design.

Mercedes-Benz buses are everywhere in Germany.

CHAPTER 9

REBUILDING

A 300 SE coupé typical of this era.

After World War II, Germany was in ruins. The Allied bombing raids destroyed many of the Daimler-Benz plants. Sindelfingen was 85 percent destroyed and Gaggenau 80 percent. Untertürkheim, Berlin, and Mannheim – all had been bombed. The company's first order of business was to put people to work rebuilding the plants. By 1950, Mercedes-Benz was producing more cars than at any time before the war; recovery was on its way.

Headquarters, engineering, and testing were centered in Untertürkheim, near Stuttgart; engines and transmissions were also manufactured there. Passenger car chassis and bodies were made in Sindelfingen. Trucks and buses were produced in Mannheim, and the Unimog all-purpose truck in Gaggenau. The Marienfelde plant in Berlin was the last to be rebuilt, and stationary diesel engine production began in 1950.

**1965 Model 600
Luxury Limousine**
Built 1964-1981
V8 engine
6.3-liter
250 hp at 4000 rpm
Top speed: 125 mph

The 220 and 300 were the first new models designed after the war. The 300 (3-liter, 6-cylinder) returned Mercedes to its international clientele, becoming the first new luxury car. This model lasted well into the 1970s and was the basis for the current S-Class cars.

New models were added in the coming years, and heads of state were once again seen driving and being driven in Mercedes-Benz automobiles.

A 280 SE coupé,
the mid-class car of the post-war years.

A special 1965 model 600
built for Pope Paul VI. Note
the papal crest on the door
and the single seat in back.

CHAPTER 10

THE 300 SL: A SPORTS CAR LEGEND

Mercedes-Benz's first entry into the racing world after the war came in 1952 with the 300 SL. Built to meet a 3000 cc maximum engine displacement rule, the 6-cylinder, 2996-cc engine produced 173 hp at 5200 rpm. The rounded body and gull-wing doors caused much comment at the first competition entered. The steering wheel came off to allow the driver to get in and out through these airplane-type doors. The car did well in its first outing at the Mille Miglia, placing second and fourth. Victories included the Prize of Berne (first, second, and third places), Le Mans (first and second), the German Grand Prix (first, second, third, and fourth), and the Carrera Panamericana in Mexico (1st and 2nd).

In 1954, the 300 SL coupé was produced as a road car and received spectacular reviews at its opening in New York. Production lasted only three years; celebrities and sports car enthusiasts from all over the world waited in line to buy it. In 1957 a convertible was produced with more conventional doors that provided much easier access. Both cars were powered by a 6-cylinder, 2.996-liter engine that produced 215 hp at 5800 rpm and an approximate top speed of 155 mph.

The 1952 model 300 SL racing car. Shown with its markings for the Carrera Panamericana race in Mexico.

The 1954 model 300 SL coupé.
Only 1,400 were produced from 1954 to 1957.
The dream car of the fifties, it is still a highly prized collector's car.

A 1960 model 300 SL convertible. Mercedes-Benz reports that 1,858
were produced from 1957 to 1963.

CHAPTER 11

THE SL SPORTS LEGEND CONTINUES

In 1955 a 190 SL touring sports car became available as a coupé with a removable hard top. This "little brother" to the 300 SL had a 4-cylinder, 1.897-liter engine that produced 105 hp at 5700 rpm for a top speed of 106 mph.

In 1963, the 230 SL convertible was introduced to replace the 190 SL. Its 6-cylinder, 2.3-liter engine produced 150 hp at 5500 rpm for a top speed of 125 mph. The model was famous for its "pagoda roof." This hard top detached and could be removed, leaving a traditional rag-top convertible. This roof has become the hallmark of the SL and is found on the 1990 models today. The year 1990 saw two new models of the SL: the 300 (3-liter) and 500 (5-liter). Priced at $75,000 and $85,000 respectively, they cannot be obtained easily. Mercedes dealers report that all models have been sold two years in advance.

Since the 1930s, Mercedes-Benz has used a simple model system for naming and numbering their cars. The numbers usually indicate engine capacity: 190 for 1.9 liters, 300 for 3.0 liters, and so forth. The letters designate the type of car: D for diesel, E for *Einspritz* (fuel injection gasoline engine), C for coupé and T for station wagon. Some letters are used for more than one type: L for lightweight or long, and S for sport or super. This

A 1964 model 230 SL convertible. First introduced in 1963, its styling made it a hallmark among grand touring cars.

A 1972 model 450 SL. This successor to the 230 series came with a 4.5-liter engine that met U.S. emission requirements.

Λ 1990 model 300 SL convertible. Today's version of this classic car follows the crisp lines and pagoda roof of a 40-year tradition.

1990 Mercedes-Benz 300 SL-24

6-cylinder
2960 cc
170 hp at 6300 rpm
Top speed: 150 mph

leads to some confusion. The 300 SL then is a 3-liter light, sports car. The 300 SE is a 3-liter, fuel-injected, super (or large) sedan. Two entirely different cars with very similar model numbers! Confusion also arises when Daimler-Benz deviates from this system. On some cars, the number is used as a model number, and the engine capacity follows: the 190 E-2.4 is a compact sedan with a 2.4-liter engine.

CHAPTER 12

COMPACT AND MID-CLASS CARS FOR THE 1990S

The Mercedes product line for the 1990s lists 54 models, only some of which are represented here. Among these are compact models, such as the 190 and mid-size autos including the 300 CE-24.

The so-called compact Mercedes comes in eight models. It can be powered by either diesel or gasoline engines of 4, 5, or 6 cylinders. The range of engine sizes and top speeds varies from 1997 cc/100 mph to 2498 cc/147 mph. The car may be smaller, but the quality, performance, and price are still Mercedes-Benz.

The mid-size or standard models include a dizzying variety of 23 different cars. Offered are coupés, sedans, and station wagons with either diesel or gasoline power. Engine size and top speed vary from the model 200 rated at 1990 cc/117 mph to the 300 CE-24 shown here and rated at 2960 cc/ 150 mph.

If any Mercedes could be called small it would be this 190 D diesel.

This 300 CE-24 has a 6-cylinder engine of 2960 cc. Top speed is reported as 150 mph.

The *Guinness Book of World Records* cites a Mercedes as the "world's most durable car." At the time of that citation, the car had clocked 1,184,880 miles and was still traveling. Mercedes is famous for long-lasting quality. Studies show that during the decade of the 1980s, Mercedes held their resale value better than any other line of cars sold in America.

CHAPTER 13

S-CLASS: THE BIG MERCEDES

The top-of-the-line Mercedes is the 560 SE. This huge car is used by presidents, kings, and world leaders from all nations.

Left: A 1990 model 260 SE is the smallest and least expensive of the S-class cars.

Ask someone to describe a Mercedes, and they will probably say "big, fast, luxury car." Those four words give a perfect description of Mercedes' top-of-the-line S models.

For the 1990s, Mercedes offers 12 models in this class. They are big cars. Really big. And they set a world standard for elegance, luxury, and engineering excellence.

Mercedes-Benz class luxury includes heated seats, electro-pneumatically adjusted backrest, headlight wiper/washers (with heated water), anti-lock braking system (which Mercedes pioneered), electrically operated interior sunshades (to keep the car cool when it is parked), electrically adjustable steering column and seats (which can be programmed into memory for different drivers), and, of course, all that space!

S-class cars start with the 260 SE (pictured left), powered by a 6-cylinder engine of 2697 cc. Biggest of the big cars is the 560 SE (pictured above) with an 8-cylinder engine of 5547 cc. Top speeds are reported respectively as 128 mph and 156 mph.

CHAPTER 14

MERCEDES-BENZ: IMPORTANT DATES

1834 Gottlieb Daimler is born in Schorndorf, Germany.

1834 Eilhard Mitscherlich develops "benzine" (gasoline).

1844 Karl Benz is born near Karlsruhe, Germany.

1867 Nicholas August Otto exhibits his first atmospheric gas engine.

1871 Germany becomes a united country under Kaiser Wilhelm I.

1881 Daimler "retires" to Cannstatt.

1883 Daimler builds and patents his first high-speed, four-cycle gasoline engines.

1883 Karl Benz founds Benz & Co.

1885 Daimler is issued a patent for a gasoline-powered bicycle (motorcycle).

1885 Benz patent motorcar is completed.

1886 Daimler installs engine in boat.

1888 Berta Benz and sons drive to Pforzheim and back.

1888 Daimler develops one-cylinder motor for airship

1899 Zeppelin uses Daimler engine in his dirigible airships.

1890 DMG (Daimler Motoren-Gesellschaft, A.G.) is founded.

1894 First automobile race is held from Paris to Rouen, France.

1894 Benz Victoria, the first four-wheel Benz car, is built.

1895 Paris-Bordeaux-Paris race (732 miles) is completed in 90 hours.

1895 The first American automobiles are built.

1896 Benz delivery truck is built.

1899 Benz & Co. becomes Benz & Cie.

1900 Gottlieb Daimler dies.

1901 Mercedes is introduced by Daimler.

1901 World speed record of 49.4 mph over 1 mile at Nice is set by a 35 hp Mercedes.

1902 Mercedes with 40 hp reaches 51.6 mph.

1904 From a flying start, 90-hp Mercedes is clocked at 97.2 mph over 1 km.

1905 Mercedes with two 60-hp engines sets a record of 109.6 mph at Daytona Beach.

1909 Blitzen Benz racing car is introduced.

1909 Benz & Cie. patents the diesel engine.

1914-1918 World War I. Car production halts in both companies to support the war effort.

1922 Mercedes sports car comes with supercharger design by Ferdinand Porsche.

1924 Benz introduces the diesel truck.

1926 Companies merge, forming Daimler-Benz, A.G.

1929 Karl Benz dies.

1933 Adolf Hitler is elected Chancellor of Germany.

1934 W25 racing car wins 16 major races.

1936 Mercedes-Benz introduces the first diesel passenger car.

1938 W125 sets land speed record of 271 mph.

1939 T80 land record car is built and tested but never raced due to start of war.

1939-1945 World War II. Car production is halted. Daimler-Benz produces tank and aircraft engines during the war.

1948-1950 Daimler-Benz works to rebuild bombed plants in Stuttgart, Mannheim, Gaggenau, and Berlin.

1948 Production on the Unimog all-purpose truck is begun in Gaggenau.

1949 Germany is officially divided into two countries: East and West.

1952 300 SL is the first racing car introduced after the war.

1954 300 SL coupé is announced to rave reviews in New York.

1957 300 SL convertible is produced to replace the coupé.

1954 W196 racing car begins a two-year winning streak with 10 Grand Prix victories.

1955 Mercedes-Benz retires from racing.

1961 The Berlin Wall goes up, dividing the city into East and West.

1963 230 SL is introduced to replace the 190 and 300 models.

1987 Mercedes-Benz returns to racing.

1989 The Berlin wall is torn down.

1990 Germany is reunited into one country.

GLOSSARY

A.G. – German for "limited" or "incorporated"

benzine – an early name for gasoline

cabriolet (CAB-ree-o-lay) – A car with a canvas top that can be folded down, a convertible

cc – cubic centimeters. The amount of space in the engine cylinders. The larger the number of cc's, the larger the engine and power. 1000 cc = 1 liter

coach builder – a person or company that built carriages, and later car bodies

coupé – a small sedan usually with only two doors

D – diesel engine

diesel – a more efficient type of engine patented by and named for Rudolf Diesel (1858-1913)

E – *Einsprintz* (fuel injection gasoline engine)

hp – horsepower. A measure of power of engines. Horsepower is always given at an engine speed (40 hp at 1050 rpm)

km/h – kilometers per hour. The speed of a car in kilometers. 1.6 km = 1 mile

mph – miles per hour. The speed of a car in miles.

rpm – revolutions per minute. Engine speed given in the number of complete engine cycles in one minute

Riviera – the southeast coast of France on the Mediterranean Sea

S-class – the big Mercedes cars

SL – the Mercedes-Benz sports car

Stuttgart (SHTOOT-gart) – The city in Germany where the Daimler-Benz headquarters is located

T – station wagon model car

INDEX

This book may be kept

FOURTEEN DAYS

A fine will be charged for each day the book is kept overtime.

APR 2 3 1998			
NOV 3 2004			
GAYLORD 142			PRINTED IN U.S.A.